T0052298

HUMANOID ROBOTS

RUNNING INTO THE FUTURE

BY KATHRYN CLAY

Consultant:
Barbara J. Fox
Professor Emerita
North Carolina State University

CAPSTONE PRESS
a capstone imprint

Blazers Books are published by Capstone Press,
1710 Roe Crest Drive, North Mankato, Minnesota 56003
www.capstonepub.com

Library of Congress Cataloging-in-Publication Data
Clay, Kathryn.
Humanoid robots : running into the future / by Kathryn Clay.
pages cm—(Blazers. The world of robots)
Audience: Age 8–10.
Audience: Grades K–3.
Includes bibliographical references and index.
Summary: "Describes the past, present, and possible future of robots that resemble
humans and human behavior"—Provided by publisher.
ISBN 978-1-4765-3975-1 (library binding)
ISBN 978-1-4765-5115-9 (paperback)
ISBN 978-1-4765-5956-8 (ebook pdf)
1. Androids—Juvenile literature. I. Title.
TJ211.2.C5385 2014
629.8'92—dc23   2013028204

Editorial Credits
Aaron Sautter, editor; Ted Williams, designer; Eric Gohl, media researcher;
Eric Manske, production specialist

Photo Credits
Alamy: The Art Gallery Collection, 8, Daniel Santos Megina, 23; AP Photo:
Jerome Favre, cover (bottom left); Getty Images: Brandi Simons, 24; NASA: 26,
27; Newscom: EPA/Andy Rain, 19, Getty Images/AFP/Yoshikazu Tsuno, 15,
Reuters/Gil Cohen Magen, 28, Reuters/Issei Kato, 21; Science Source: Peter
Menzel, 11, 13; Shutterstock: Denis Klimov, cover (bottom right), Ivan Nikulin,
cover (top), KUCO, 7; Wikipedia: Gnsin, 4, Vanillase, 16

TABLE OF CONTENTS

Lifelike humanoid robots called actroids were first built in Japan in 2003.

It's a ROBOT!

A young woman walks onto a stage and waves to the crowd. Wait—that's not a person. It's a **robot**! **Humanoid** robots keep becoming more lifelike. Let's see how they have advanced over time.

robot—a machine programmed to do jobs usually performed by a person

humanoid—having a human form or characteristics

EARLY MECHANICAL PEOPLE

TALOS

People have imagined humanlike machines for thousands of years. One Greek myth describes a giant bronze statue named Talos. In the story, the Greek gods brought Talos to life to guard an island against invaders.

myth—a story told by people in ancient times

ROBOT FACT

In the late 1400s, inventor and artist Leonardo da Vinci designed and drew plans for a robotic knight.

Talos

The Scribe

AUTOMATONS

In the 1700s Pierre Jaquet-Droz and his sons built **automatons** using springs, gears, and other parts. The mechanical dolls played music, drew pictures, and wrote letters.

automaton—a mechanical device designed to follow a set of instructions

ROBOT FACT

The three Jaquet-Droz automatons were called The Musician, The Draftsman, and The Scribe.

LEARNING TO WALK AND TALK

WABOT-1

Scientists began building more advanced humanoid robots in the 1970s. They also began giving robots **artificial intelligence**. The first robot to walk on two legs was WABOT-1 in 1970. It could speak several words in Japanese.

artificial intelligence—the ability of a machine to think like a person

ROBOT FACT

WASUBOT was built in 1985. It was based on WABOT-1 and could play music on an organ.

WABOT-1

COG

In 1993 scientists began building a robot called Cog as a research project. The robot learns to do things by watching and imitating people. Cog has also helped scientists learn how people respond to humanlike machines.

ROBOT FACT

Like Cog, the iCub robot helps scientists in Europe research how children learn. This humanoid robot thinks and acts much like a 3½-year-old child.

Cog

Almost Human

QRIO

In the early 2000s, the Sony Company developed a robot called QRIO. It had more humanlike movement. Using 38 different motors, it could walk, run, sing, and dance.

ROBOT FACT

QRIO was going to be sold to the public. But Sony stopped working on the robots in 2006.

QRIO

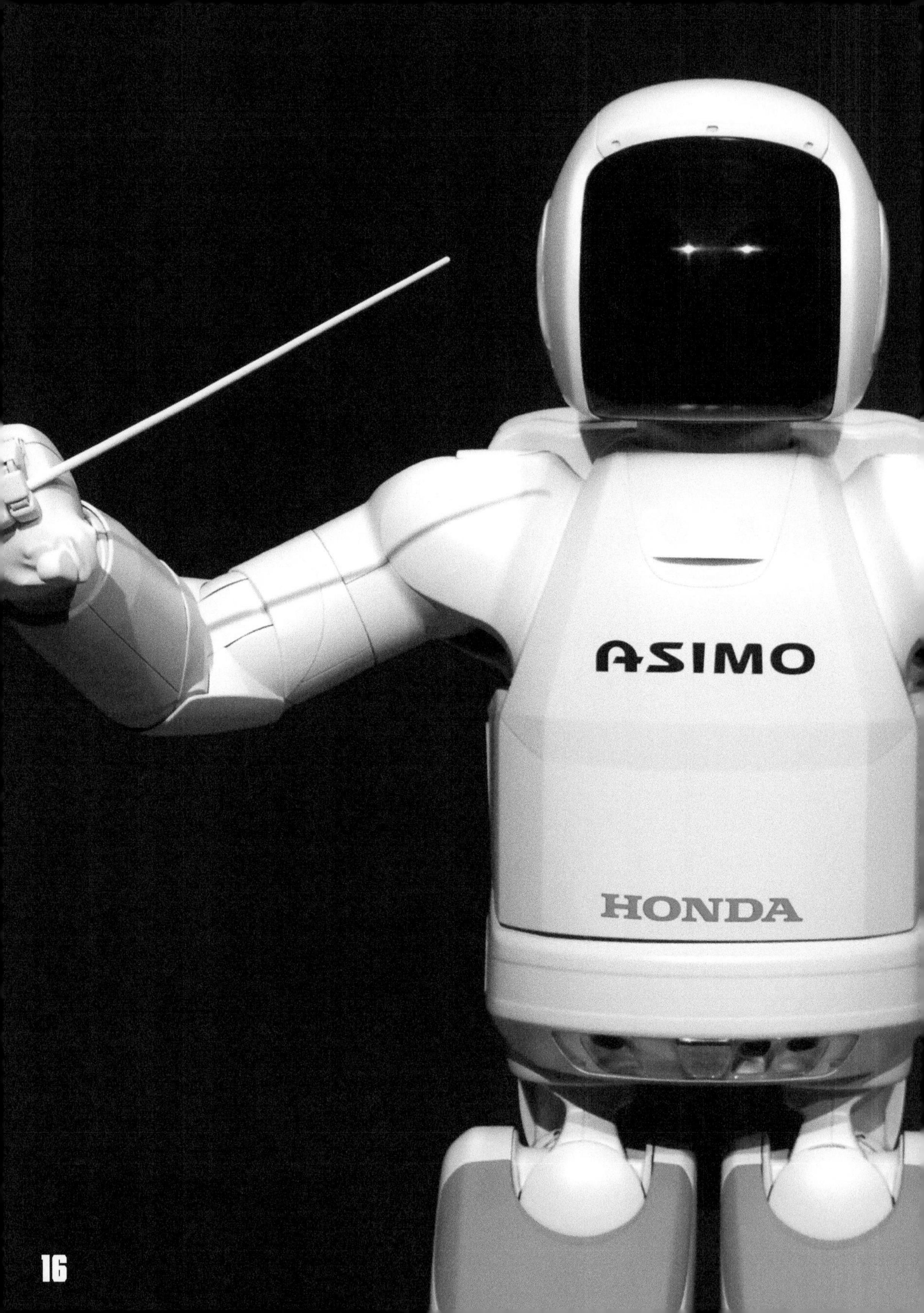
ASIMO
HONDA

ROBOT FACT
ASIMO stands for "Advanced Step in Innovative Mobility."

ASIMO

The Honda Company first introduced ASIMO in 2000. ASIMO recognizes faces and certain hand movements. In 2012 ASIMO was given more realistic movement. The robot now runs and climbs stairs.

REPLIEE Q1EXPO

Repliee Q1Expo was introduced in 2007. It was one of the most lifelike robots in the world. The **android** had soft artificial "skin." It could blink its eyes and even seemed to breathe.

android—a robot that looks, thinks, and acts very similar to a human being

ROBOT FACT

Science fiction stories often feature realistic androids. The character Data on the TV show *Star Trek: The Next Generation* was a humanlike robot.

Repliee Q1Expo

HUMANOIDS AT WORK

ROBOT RECEPTIONISTS

Humanoid robots are starting to show up in public places. The Saya android has worked as both a receptionist and a teacher. Saya uses 700 phrases to speak with people.

receptionist—someone who works in an office to greet visitors and answer phone calls

ROBOT FACT

The robot Showa Hanako is used to train dentistry students in Japan. This realistic robot blinks, sneezes, and coughs like a real patient.

REEM

The REEM service robot was designed for many uses. It provides useful information and guides visitors in public places. REEM can also be **programmed** to entertain people or carry small packages.

 program—to enter a series of instructions in a computer language

ROBOT FACT

The 2004 movie *I, Robot* features a character with an advanced robotic arm.

ROBOTIC LIMBS

Researching humanoid robots also helps people with missing limbs. Robotic arms and legs help them live normal lives. The newest robotic limbs work with a person's own nerves and muscles.

limb—a part of the body used in moving or grasping; arms and legs are limbs

nerve—a thin fiber that carries messages between the brain and other parts of the body

ROBONAUT 2

Humanoid robots are even used in space. Robonaut 2 was sent to the *International Space Station* in 2011. It currently performs dull, repetitive tasks. But Robonaut 2 may be used for more dangerous missions in the future.

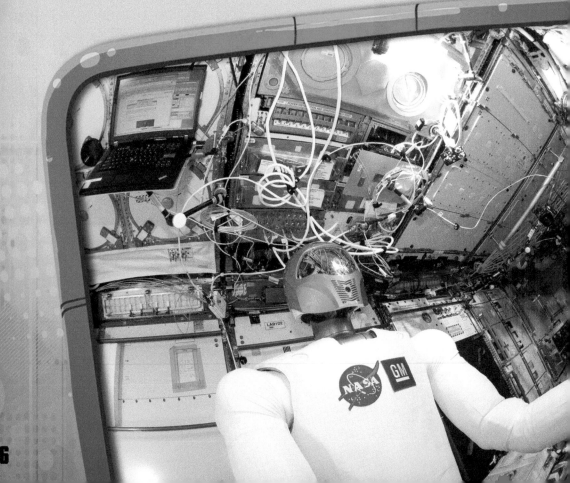

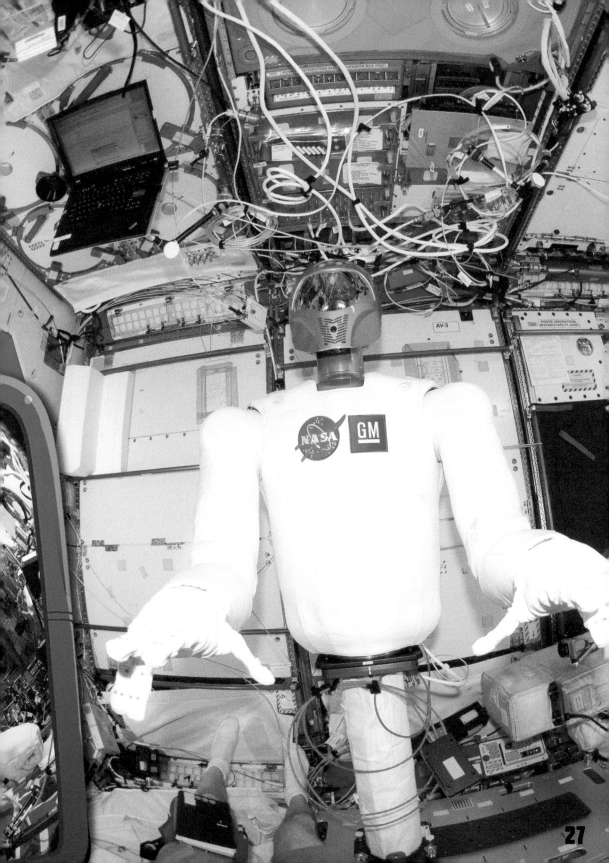

ROBOT FACT

The Jetsons was a cartoon show that featured a robot maid named Rosie. She cooked, cleaned, and kept the family's house running smoothly.

LOOKING TO THE FUTURE

Scientists continue to make robots more lifelike. One day robots may be a large part of people's daily lives. Androids may work in hospitals, schools, or shopping malls. The future holds endless possibilities.

GLOSSARY

android (AN-droid)—a robot that looks, thinks, and acts very similar to a human being

artificial intelligence (ar-tih-FISH-uhl in-TEL-uh-juhnts)—the ability of a machine to think like a person

automaton (aw-TAH-muh-tahn)—a mechanical device designed to follow a set of instructions

humanoid (HYOO-muh-noyd)—having a human form or characteristics

limb (LIM)—a part of the body used in moving or grasping; arms and legs are limbs

myth (MITH)—a story told by people in ancient times

nerve (NURV)—a thin fiber that carries messages between the brain and other parts of the body

program (PROH-gram)—to enter a series of instructions in a computer language

receptionist (ree-SEP-shun-ist)—someone who works in an office to greet visitors and answer phone calls

robot (ROH-bot)—a machine programmed to do jobs usually performed by a person

READ MORE

Brasch, Nicolas. *Robots and Artificial Intelligence.* The Technology Behind. Mankato, Minn.: Smart Apple Media, 2011.

Gifford, Clive. *Robots.* Discover Science. Boston: Kingfisher, 2011.

Hyland, Tony. *Robot World.* Fast Facts. Mankato, Minn.: Sea-to-Sea Publications, 2012.

INTERNET SITES

FactHound offers a safe, fun way to find Internet sites related to this book. All of the sites on FactHound have been researched by our staff.

Here's all you do:

Visit *www.facthound.com*

Type in this code: 9781476539751

Check out projects, games and lots more at
www.capstonekids.com

INDEX